hot & spicy

hot & spicy

TIME
LIFE
BOOKS

Alexandria, Virginia

Time-Life Books is a division of Time Life Inc.

TIME LIFE INC.
Chairman and CEO   Jim Nelson
President and COO   Steven L. Janas

TIME-LIFE TRADE PUBLISHING
Vice President and Publisher   Neil Levin
Senior Director of Acquisitions and Editorial Resources   Jennifer Pearce
Director of New Product Development   Carolyn Clark
Director of Marketing   Inger Forland
Director of Trade Sales   Dana Hobson
Director of Custom Publishing   John Lalor
Director of Special Markets   Robert Lombardi
Director of Design   Kate L. McConnell

HOT & SPICY
Project Manager   Jennie Halfant
Technical Specialist   Monika Lynde

This edition first published in the U.K. in 2000 by Hamlyn
Octopus Publishing Group Limited
2–4 Heron Quays
London E14 4JP

Printed in China
10 9 8 7 6 5 4 3 2 1

Library of Congress Cataloging-in-Publication Data
Hot & spicy: over 60 simple recipes for elegant home cooking.
    p. cm.
  Includes index.
  ISBN 0-7370-2054-7
    1. Cookery, International. 2. Spices. I. Time-Life Books.

  TX725.A1 H582 2000
  641.59--dc21
                                    00-023456

Notes
1 Milk should be whole milk unless otherwise stated.
2 Fresh herbs should be used unless otherwise stated. If unavailable, use dried herbs as an alternative but only half the amount stated.
3 Pepper should be freshly ground black pepper unless otherwise stated; season according to taste.
4 Do not refreeze a dish that has been frozen previously.

contents

6

introduction

There is no doubt that hot, spicy food is addictive. Once you have a taste for it, dishes cooked without hot spices can taste disappointingly bland. The recipes in this collection cater for all levels of taste, ranging from the mildly spiced Piperade on page 24 to Chiles Stuffed with Curried Crab on page 28, a red alert recipe designed for seasoned chile fanatics.

In the past, attempts to preserve food often involved generous amounts of pepper and other potent seasonings. Such seasonings were also used to disguise the not too savory taste of meats and other foods served past their sell-by dates! Although spices can add fragrance, flavor, and color to other foods, some are chosen primarily for their heat and strength: the three most important hot spices being chile, mustard, and pepper (see below). Other sources of heat are listed on page 7. If you find your mouth and throat burning from too much hot spice (chiles are the worst offender), then rice, sliced banana, or milk may help a little.

Chiles

These are the most powerful of all the hot spices and should be treated with respect. Chiles are used extensively in the cuisines of hot climates, as the hot chiles cause the body to perspire and thus, cool it down. They originated in the Amazon region of South America and in Mexico and were brought back to Spain by Columbus, from where they reached Portugal. When the Portuguese established their trading posts in southern India, they took the chile with them, which is how the chile's heat first found its way into Indian curry dishes. There are over 300 varieties of chile, ranging from subtle to incendiary flavors. On the whole, the hottest are the tiny ones (the habanero is the most powerful of all), and the seeds and inner membrane, the hottest part; discard them for a milder flavor. The volatile oils in chiles can sting and cause discomfort, so wear rubber gloves when preparing them, and do not touch your eyes. Chiles are sold both fresh and dried. Paprika, which may be hot or mild, hot cayenne pepper, crushed chili flakes and chili powder are all prepared from chiles.

Mustard

This is prepared from the seeds of three plants of the cabbage family. These seeds, which may be white, brown, or black, are the basis of all prepared mustards, which range in strength from hot and sharp, like English mustard, to the mild, sweet, and smooth American mustard. To make a powerful English mustard to serve with roast beef, mix the powder with a little cold water and leave for 10–15 minutes before serving. Mustard loses its pungency with heat, which is why large quantities can be added to sauces without overpowering them. French mustards are sold made up rather than in powder form. Dijon is a smooth, pale yellow mustard with a subtle flavor of varying strength. Bordeaux is dark brown and aromatic, with a sweet-sour taste. Meaux mustard, also called moutarde à l'ancienne, is grainy and mild.

"Variety's the very spice of life that gives it all its flavor."

William Cowper

Pepper

Black, white, and green peppercorns all come from the same plant, *Piper nigrum*, a climbing vine native to the south of India, and first brought to Europe in the fifth century BC. The berries are green before they ripen, when they turn bright red. Black peppercorns are picked unripe and then dried in the sun. White peppercorns are the red berries ripened on the vine, then washed, fermented, dehusked, and dried. For maximum flavor, black and white peppercorns should be ground in a pepper mill, as needed, rather than bought ready-ground. Black pepper has the more rounded, aromatic flavor, but some people like to use white pepper in pale-colored dishes, where black flecks may look out of place. The soft, squashy green peppercorns are also picked before they ripen and are packed in vinegar, brine, or water, or they may be air-dried.

Spices, Condiments & Sauces

Allspice: Also called Jamaica pepper, this hard, brown berry tastes of cloves, cinnamon, and nutmeg; used in spice mixtures, marinades, and some sweet dishes.

Five-spice powder: A Chinese spice mixture made from cinnamon, cloves, fennel, star anise, and Szechuan pepper.

Garam masala: An Indian blend of hot and aromatic spices, usually containing coriander seeds, cumin, cinnamon, cardamom seeds, nutmeg, and cloves.

Horseradish sauce: A pungent condiment prepared from grated horseradish root, and is one of Britain's traditional accompaniments to roast beef. Wasabi, sometimes known as Japanese horseradish, is unrelated to true horseradish.

Salsa cruda: Also known as Wet Chile Mixture. Variations of this uncooked chile and tomato sauce are found throughout Latin America and the Caribbean.

Sambal oelek: An Indonesian sauce made with crushed chiles, salt, and vinegar.

Tabasco sauce: A fiery pepper sauce made in Louisiana, from a type of chile associated in particular with Creole and Tex-Mex cooking.

Thai green and red curry pastes: Two hot Far Eastern curry pastes, the green and red element depending on the type of chiles used.

Worcestershire sauce: A British adaptation of an Indian recipe, made from a secret formula and dating back to the days of the Raj.

8

thai red curry paste

1 Put all the ingredients in a food processor or blender, and blend to a thick paste. Or, you can pound together all the ingredients using a mortar and pestle.

2 Transfer the paste to an airtight container. It can be stored in the refrigerator for up to 3 weeks.

10 large fresh red chiles

2 teaspoons coriander seeds

2-inch piece galangal or ginger, finely chopped

1 lemon grass stalk, finely chopped

4 garlic cloves, cut in half

1 shallot, roughly chopped

1 teaspoon lime juice

2 tablespoons peanut oil

Makes about 1½ cups

Preparation time: 15 minutes

spicy peanut dressing

1 Chop the creamed coconut and place it in a small saucepan with the milk. Set over a low heat for about 2 minutes, stirring constantly, until the coconut melts and forms a paste with the milk.

2 Transfer the coconut mixture to a food processor or blender. Add the onion, garlic, peanut butter, sugar, soy sauce, ground cumin, and ground red chile, and season to taste with salt and pepper. Purée until smooth, then scrape into a small bowl. Cover and set aside until needed.

2 tablespoons creamed coconut

¼ cup milk

½ small onion, roughly chopped

1 garlic clove, crushed

¼ cup smooth peanut butter

1 teaspoon soft light brown sugar

2 teaspoons soy sauce

½ teaspoon ground cumin

½ teaspoon ground red chile

salt and pepper

Makes about ¾ cup

Preparation time: 10 minutes

Cooking time: 2 minutes

salsa cruda

1 In a bowl, mix together the tomatoes, onion, chiles, cilantro, lemon juice, and sugar, with salt to taste. Store in an airtight container and serve when needed.

1 lb. (around 1½ cups) peeled, seeded, and diced tomatoes

⅓ cup chopped onion

3 medium-size mild green chiles, peeled, seeded, and diced

½ tablespoon finely chopped cilantro

1 tablespoon lemon juice

1 teaspoon sugar

salt

Makes about 2 cups

Preparation time: 10 minutes

chile oil

1 Mix together the olive oil, cilantro, and chile, and season with sea salt and pepper. Leave to infuse for 1–2 days before use. The oil will keep for months if stored in an airtight container.

¼ cup olive oil

1 tablespoon finely chopped cilantro

1 small red chile, seeded and chopped

sea salt and pepper

Makes ½ cup

Preparation time: 5 minutes plus infusing

■ Drizzle a little chile oil over savory dishes to add extra spice, or simply drizzle a little on some fresh crusty bread for a quick and tasty snack.

chili bean & pepper soup •

cauliflower, cilantro & coconut soup •

mexican soup with avocado salsa •

polenta salad with goat cheese & chile oil •

watercress & pomegranate salad •

chiles rellenos •

spicy nachos with cheese •

vegetable samosas •

pakora •

stuffed green peppers •

piperade •

chili bean dip •

fire
starters

chili bean & pepper soup

1 Heat the oil in a large pot, and fry the onion and garlic until soft but not colored. Stir in the peppers and chiles and fry for a few minutes. Stir in the stock and tomato juice or purée, tomato paste, sun-dried tomato paste, chili sauce, kidney beans, and cilantro. Bring to a boil, cover, lower the heat, and simmer for 30 minutes.

2 Let the soup cool slightly, then purée in a food processor or blender until smooth. Return the soup to the pot, and taste and adjust the seasoning, adding a little extra chili sauce, if wanted. Bring to a boil and pour into warmed soup bowls. Stir a little sour cream into each one, and garnish with strips of lime zest. Serve with tortilla chips.

■ For an interesting variation, use chipotle chiles—a smoked version of jalapeños. They lose none of their heat through the smoking process.

2 tablespoons sunflower oil

1 large onion, finely chopped

4 garlic cloves, finely chopped

2 red bell peppers, cored, seeded, and diced

2 red chiles, seeded and finely chopped

1 quart vegetable stock

3 cups tomato juice or tomato purée

1 tablespoon tomato paste

1 tablespoon sun-dried tomato paste

2 tablespoons sweet chili sauce, or more to taste

a 14-oz. can red kidney beans, drained and rinsed

2 tablespoons finely chopped cilantro

⅓ cup sour cream

salt and pepper

zest of 1 lime, cut into strips, to garnish

tortilla chips, to serve

Serves 6

Preparation time: 20 minutes

Cooking time: 40 minutes

14

cauliflower, cilantro & coconut soup

1 Put the lemon grass, sliced ginger, lime leaves, cilantro stalks, and vegetable stock into a pot. Bring to a boil, cover, and simmer for 30 minutes.

2 Heat the oil in a large pot, add the onion, garlic, grated ginger, and chile and fry for 5 minutes, until lightly golden. Add the turmeric and cauliflower, and fry for a further 5 minutes.

3 Strain the lemon grass stock and add it to the cauliflower mixture. Stir in the coconut milk and cilantro, bring to a boil, and simmer very gently for 15–20 minutes, until the cauliflower is cooked through and tender. Add the lemon juice, season to taste with salt and pepper, and serve in bowls garnished with a drizzle of sesame oil and a few cilantro leaves.

2 lemon grass stalks, roughly chopped

4 slices fresh ginger

4 kaffir lime leaves, bruised

2 cilantro stalks, bruised

1 quart vegetable stock

2 tablespoons sunflower oil

1 onion, thinly sliced

2 garlic cloves, chopped

1 teaspoon grated fresh ginger

1 red chile, seeded and sliced

1 teaspoon ground turmeric

1 cauliflower, trimmed and divided into small florets

a 13-oz. can coconut milk

2 tablespoons finely chopped cilantro

1 tablespoon lemon juice

salt and pepper

To Garnish:

sesame oil

cilantro

Serves 4
Preparation time: 20 minutes
Cooking time: about 1 hour

2 tablespoons sunflower oil

1 large onion, chopped

2 garlic cloves, crushed

2 teaspoons ground coriander

1 teaspoon ground cumin

1 red bell pepper, cored, seeded, and diced

2 red chiles, seeded and chopped

a 14-oz. can red kidney beans, drained and rinsed

3 cups tomato juice

2 tablespoons chili sauce, or to taste

1 heaped cup tortilla chips, crushed

salt and pepper

extra tortilla chips, to garnish

Avocado Salsa:

1 small ripe avocado

4 scallions, finely chopped

1 tablespoon lemon juice

1 tablespoon finely chopped cilantro

Serves 6

Preparation time: 20 minutes

Cooking time: 45 minutes

1 Heat the oil in a large pot, add the onion, garlic, spices, red bell pepper, and chiles, and fry gently for 10 minutes. Add the beans, tomato juice, and chili sauce, and bring to a boil. Cover and simmer over a low heat for 30 minutes.

2 Meanwhile, make the avocado salsa. Peel, pit, and finely dice the avocado and combine with the scallions, lemon juice, and cilantro. Season to taste with salt and pepper, cover with plastic wrap, and set aside until needed

3 Put the soup into a food processor with the tortilla chips, and purée until smooth. Return to the pot, season to taste with salt and pepper, and heat through. Serve the soup in bowls topped with the avocado salsa and extra tortilla chips.

mexican soup with avocado salsa

chiles rellenos

1 Cut a small slit in each chile and remove the seeds, leaving the stems on. Dry well with paper towels. Place a stick of cheese inside each chile. Beat the egg whites until stiff. Lightly beat the egg yolks and fold in the whites. Dip the chiles in the egg mixture, then roll them in the flour to coat evenly.

2 Heat the oil in a deep-fat fryer to 350°F or until a cube of bread browns in 30 seconds. Deep-fry the chiles until brown, turning occasionally. Drain on paper towels, then place in a shallow flameproof dish or cast-iron pan, and top with chili sauce and cheese. Place under a hot broiler to melt the cheese until golden before serving.

6 large fresh poblano or New Mexico chiles, skinned (see page 28)

6 oz. Cheddar cheese, cut into six equal sticks

3 eggs, separated

½ cup all-purpose flour

vegetable oil, for deep-frying

To Serve:

a little Chile Sauce (see page 19)

½ cup grated Cheddar cheese

Serves 3–6
Preparation time: 20 minutes
Cooking time: 15 minutes

an 8-oz. bag of tortilla chips

1 cup grated Cheddar cheese

Chile Sauce:

2 tablespoons vegetable oil

1 onion, chopped

2 garlic cloves, crushed

4 large tomatoes, skinned, seeded, and chopped

2 jalapeño chiles, seeded and chopped

pinch of dried oregano

pinch of ground cumin

salt and pepper

To Garnish:

2 scallions, cut into strips

1 red chile, seeded, and cut into strips

Serves 4–6
Preparation time: 20 minutes
Cooking time: 25–30 minutes

1 First make the chile sauce. Heat the oil in a small pan and sauté the onion and garlic until soft and golden, stirring occasionally. Add the tomatoes, chiles, oregano, and cumin, and season to taste with salt and pepper. Bring to a boil, lower the heat, and simmer gently for about 15 minutes, or until the sauce is thickened and reduced.

2 Arrange the tortilla chips in a large ovenproof dish and spoon the chili sauce over the top. Sprinkle with the grated Cheddar and cook in a preheated oven, 350°F, for 10–15 minutes, or until the cheese melts and starts to bubble.

3 Meanwhile, soak the scallion and chile strips in very cold water for 5–10 minutes to make them curl. Serve the nachos garnished with the scallion and chile curls.

spicy nachos with cheese

vegetable samosas

1 First make the pastry. Sift the flour and salt into a bowl. Rub in the ghee or butter until the mixture resembles breadcrumbs. Add the water and knead to a very smooth dough. Cover and chill while preparing the filling.

2 To make the filling, heat the oil in a large pan and add the mustard seeds. Leave for a few seconds until they start to pop, then add the onion and fry for 5 minutes, until golden. Add the chiles, turmeric, ginger, and salt to taste, and fry for 3 minutes; if the mixture starts sticking to the pan, add 1½ teaspoons water and stir well. Add the peas, stir thoroughly, and cook for 2 minutes. Add the potatoes and cilantro, stir well, and cook for 1 minute. Stir in the lemon juice. Allow to cool slightly.

3 Divide the pastry into 8 pieces. Dust with flour and roll each piece out into a thin round, then cut each round in half. Carefully fold each half into a cone and brush the seam with water to seal.

4 Fill the cone with a spoonful of filling (do not overfill), dampen the top edge, and seal firmly. Heat the oil and deep-fry the samosas until crisp and golden. Serve hot or warm, with the mint and yogurt sauce or a cooling raita.

1 cup all-purpose flour

¼ teaspoon salt

2 tablespoons ghee or butter

2–3 tablespoons water

oil, for deep-frying

Mint & Yogurt Sauce (see page 38), to serve

Filling:

1 tablespoon vegetable oil

1 teaspoon mustard seeds

1 small onion, finely chopped

2 green chiles, minced

¼ teaspoon ground turmeric

1 teaspoon finely chopped fresh ginger

1 cup frozen peas

1 cup cooked potatoes, diced

½ tablespoon finely chopped cilantro

1 tablespoon lemon juice

salt

Serves 4

Preparation time: 15 minutes plus cooling and chilling

Cooking time: about 30 minutes

pakora

1 Sift the flour, salt, and ground red pepper into a bowl. Stir in enough water, about ⅔ cup, to make a thick batter, and beat well until smooth. Leave to stand for about 30 minutes.

2 Stir the chiles and cilantro into the batter, then add the vegetable oil. Add the onion rings and coat thickly with batter.

3 Heat the oil in a deep pan, drop in the onion rings, and deep-fry until they are crisp and golden. Remove from the pan with a slotted spoon, drain on paper towels, and keep warm.

4 Dip the spinach leaves into the batter and deep-fry in the same way, adding more oil to the pan, if necessary. Repeat the process with the potato slices. Serve hot with a selection of chutneys.

1 cup gram (besan) flour

1 teaspoon salt

½ teaspoon ground red pepper

2 green chiles, finely chopped

1 tablespoon finely chopped cilantro

1 tablespoon vegetable oil plus extra for deep-frying

2 onions, sliced into rings

8 small spinach leaves, washed

2–3 potatoes, parboiled and sliced

Serves 4

Preparation time: 20 minutes plus standing

Cooking time: about 30 minutes

■ Gram flour is made from chickpeas and is suitable for people allergic to gluten, a component of wheat products.

1. Place the peppers in a large pot and cover with cold water. Bring to a boil, then reduce the heat and simmer gently until the peppers are tender but still firm. Drain and leave to cool.

2. To prepare the stuffing, heat the oil in a large frying pan and add the onion, garlic, and chiles. Fry gently over a low heat until the onion is soft and golden brown. Add the ground beef and stir well. Continue cooking over a low heat until well browned. Add the lemon zest and cooked rice. Season to taste with salt, pepper, and paprika. Cook gently for 5 minutes and then stir in the chopped chives.

3. Slice the tops off the peppers and scoop out the seeds. Fill with the stuffing and place in a greased baking pan. Surround with the tomatoes and bake in a preheated oven, 350°F, for about 20 minutes. Garnish with snipped chives and serve hot.

4 large green bell peppers

4 tomatoes, thinly sliced

salt and pepper

snipped chives, to garnish

Spicy Stuffing:

2 tablespoons vegetable oil

1 small onion, finely chopped

1 garlic clove, crushed

1–2 red chiles, seeded and finely chopped

¼ lb. ground beef

grated zest of 1 lemon

¼ cup cooked rice

pinch of paprika

a few chopped chives

Serves 4	
Preparation time: 15 minutes	
Cooking time: 45 minutes	

stuffed green peppers

1 Heat 6 tablespoons of the oil in a frying pan, add the pepper strips and sauté over a moderate heat until soft, stirring frequently. Add the onions, chile, and garlic, and fry gently for 10 minutes, stirring. Add the sugar, tomatoes, and bouquet garni, and season with salt and pepper. Cook over a low heat for a further 10 minutes, stirring occasionally. Heat the remaining olive oil in a separate pan and heat the slices of ham gently.

2 Pour the beaten eggs into a lightly oiled or greased frying pan and cook for 2–3 minutes over a very low heat without stirring.

3 Discard the bouquet garni, then stir the vegetable mixture into the eggs. Keep stirring until the eggs start to scramble and cook through. Adjust the seasoning to taste. Serve the piperade straight from the pan accompanied by the slices of ham.

piperade

■ Skin tomatoes by cutting a small cross in the base and then placing them in boiling water for about 1 minute. Drain and cool slightly. The skins should then slip off easily.

7 tablespoons olive oil

4 large red bell peppers, peeled (see page 52), seeded, and cut into thin strips

4 large onions, thinly sliced

1 hot red chile, thinly sliced

2 garlic cloves, crushed

pinch of sugar

2 lb. tomatoes, skinned, seeded, and chopped

1 bouquet garni

6 thick slices ham

6 eggs, lightly beaten

salt and pepper

Serves 6

Preparation time: 15–20 minutes

Cooking time: 25–30 minutes

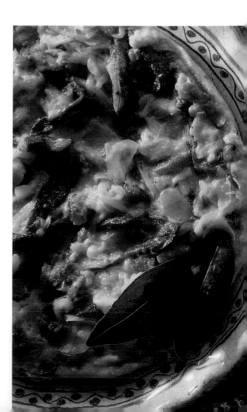

chili bean dip

1 Put the pepper flesh, half the oil, garlic, and chile in a food processor or blender, and blend until well chopped. Add the beans and paprika, and continue to blend until a coarse purée forms. Season to taste with Tabasco and salt and pepper. With the machine running, add the rest of the oil to make a thick paste.

2 Pile the bean purée into a bowl and sprinkle with the chives. Cover and refrigerate until required. Serve with fresh vegetables, corn chips, or toasted pita bread to dunk into the dip.

■ This dip is also very good served spread on bruschetta, like a pâté.

2 large red bell peppers, skinned (see page 52), halved lengthwise, and seeded

2 tablespoons olive oil

2 garlic cloves, crushed

1 red chile, seeded and finely chopped

a 14-oz. can red kidney beans, drained and rinsed

½ teaspoon paprika

dash of Tabasco sauce

salt and pepper

2 tablespoons snipped chives, to garnish

assorted fresh vegetables, corn chips, or toasted pita bread, to serve

Makes about 2 cups

Preparation time: 20 minutes plus chilling

flaming fish dishes

1 To prepare the chiles for stuffing, put them under a preheated hot broiler for 8–10 minutes, turning them occasionally, until they have softened and their skins are charred and patched with black. Remove the chiles from the broiler and leave to cool, covered with damp paper towels. (This will make their skins easier to peel.)

2 Meanwhile, prepare the stuffing. Heat the oil in a pan, add the garlic, ginger, and scallions and cook over gentle heat, stirring occasionally, for 3 minutes, until softened. Stir in the lime leaves, red curry paste, and turmeric, and cook, stirring, for 2 minutes. Remove the pan from the heat and stir in the flaked crabmeat, lime juice, and fish sauce.

3 Peel the chiles, leaving the stalks intact, and make a slit down one side of each chile from the stalk to the tip. Scrape out and discard the seeds. Stuff the chiles with the curried crabmeat mixture, place them in a single layer in a shallow ovenproof dish, and cover with foil. Cook in a preheated oven, 400°F, for 15 minutes, until they are heated through. Serve immediately.

6 red jalapeño chiles

6 green jalapeño chiles

2 tablespoons vegetable oil

2 garlic cloves, crushed

1 teaspoon grated fresh ginger

3 scallions, chopped

2 kaffir lime leaves, very finely chopped

1 tablespoon Thai Red Curry Paste (see page 8)

¼ teaspoon ground turmeric

⅔ cup fresh or canned white crabmeat, flaked

1 tablespoon lime juice

2 teaspoons Thai fish sauce

Serves 4–6

Preparation time: about 30 minutes

Cooking time: 30 minutes

chiles stuffed with curried crab

shrimp & noodles in spicy broth

1 Put the shrimp into a bowl with a pinch of salt. Mix the cornstarch to a smooth paste with the cold water, and stir into the shrimp.

2 Cook the egg noodles according to the package instructions in a large pot of lightly salted boiling water, or until just tender. Drain well and place the noodles in a large, warm serving bowl. Bring the stock to a boil and pour it over the noodles with half of the soy sauce. Keep warm.

3 Heat the oil in a wok and add the shredded scallions to flavor the oil. Add the shrimp mixture and bamboo shoots or mushrooms, and spinach. Stir a few times and then add 1½ teaspoons salt, the remaining soy sauce, and the sherry. Cook for 1–2 minutes, stirring constantly.

4 Pour the mixture over the noodles and sprinkle with sesame oil. Serve immediately, garnished with the chopped red chile and the cilantro sprigs.

½ lb. (2 cups) cooked, peeled shrimp

1 teaspoon cornstarch

1 tablespoon cold water

12 oz. egg noodles

2½ cups chicken stock

2 tablespoons light soy sauce

3 tablespoons vegetable oil

2 scallions, thinly shredded

¾ cup thinly sliced bamboo shoots or button mushrooms

2 large handfuls spinach, thinly sliced

2 tablespoons dry sherry

1–2 tablespoons sesame oil

salt

To Garnish:

1 red chile, chopped

cilantro sprigs

Serves 4
Preparation time: 15 minutes
Cooking time: 15 minutes

ginger-chile fish

1 Put the rice, water, and salt into a pot. Bring to a boil and stir once. Cover and simmer for 15 minutes, or according to the package instructions, until the rice is tender and all the liquid has been absorbed.

2 While the rice is cooking, combine all the sauce ingredients in a cup and set aside.

3 Coat the fish with flour. Heat the oil in a wok, add the fish, and fry for 3 minutes. Remove the fish and reheat the oil, then return to the pan to crisp it. Remove the fish, drain on paper towels, then transfer to a warmed serving dish. Pour the chile sauce into the wok and cook for 2 minutes, then pour this over the fish. Serve immediately with the rice.

1⅓ cups long-grain rice

1¼ cups water

½ teaspoon salt

1 lb. fish fillets (e.g., cod or flounder), cut into 2-inch slices

flour, for coating

1¼ cups vegetable oil

Ginger & Chile Sauce:

2 teaspoons finely chopped fresh ginger

1 tablespoon chopped scallion

3 tablespoons dry sherry

1 tablespoon soy sauce

2 teaspoons sugar

1 teaspoon salt

1 tablespoon chile sauce (ready-made or see page 19)

Serves 4
Preparation time: 10–15 minutes
Cooking time: about 20 minutes

1   Melt the butter in a heavy frying pan over low heat, taking care that it does not brown. Add the onion and garlic, and cook gently until softened and golden. Add the curry powder and flour, stir well, and cook gently for 2 minutes, stirring. Add the coconut milk and chile and stir to mix them thoroughly. Simmer gently for 5–10 minutes, until smooth and thickened.

2   Meanwhile, skin the fish fillets with a sharp knife. Discard the skin and arrange the fillets in a large, shallow ovenproof dish. Sprinkle the lime juice over the top.

3   Season the curry sauce to taste with salt and pepper, and pour it over the fillets. Cover the dish and cook in a preheated oven, 325°F, for about 12–15 minutes, until the fish is just cooked but still firm. Sprinkle with cilantro, and serve with boiled rice and mango chutney.

3 tablespoons butter

1 large onion, finely chopped

1 garlic clove, crushed

1 tablespoon curry powder

1 tablespoon flour

a 14-oz. can coconut milk

1 green chile, seeded and chopped

1¼ lb. white fish fillets

juice of ½ lime

salt and pepper

chopped cilantro, to garnish

To Serve:

boiled rice

mango chutney

Serves 4
Preparation time: 10 minutes
Cooking time: 25–30 minutes

fish curry

■ The word "curry" comes from the southern Indian word "kari", which means sauce. To save time, you could serve it with warmed naan bread instead of rice.

spicy fish stew

1 Heat the oil in a large, heavy pot, and gently sauté the onion, garlic, and peppers, stirring occasionally, for about 10–15 minutes, or until tender.

2 Add the tomatoes, ginger, cilantro, oregano, lime zest, chile sauce, and dried red chiles. Stir well, then simmer gently over a low heat for 10 minutes.

3 Add the monkfish and fish stock to the pot, and bring to a boil. Reduce the heat and simmer gently for 20 minutes.

4 Stir in the scallops and shrimp and cook gently for 2 minutes, until they are cooked. Season to taste with salt and pepper, and serve garnished with cilantro leaves.

3 tablespoons olive oil

1 large onion, chopped

2 garlic cloves, crushed

1 large red bell pepper, cored, seeded, and chopped

1 large yellow bell pepper, cored, seeded, and chopped

1 lb. tomatoes, peeled and chopped (around 1½ cups)

2 tablespoons finely chopped fresh ginger

1 tablespoon finely chopped cilantro

2 teaspoons chopped oregano

grated zest of 1 lime

dash of hot chile sauce

2–4 dried red chiles, chopped

2½ lb. monkfish, skinned, boned, and cut into chunks

1¼ cups fish stock

12 scallops, cut in half horizontally

½ lb. raw shrimp

salt and pepper

cilantro leaves, to garnish

Serves 6

Preparation time: 15 minutes

Cooking time: 45 minutes

stir-fried shrimp with cumin & chile

1   Heat the oil in a wok or frying pan until it is hot, then stir-fry the cumin seeds and turmeric for 30 seconds. Add the onion and stir fry for about 5 minutes, until it starts to brown. Add the pepper, tomatoes, and chiles, and season to taste with salt. Stir-fry for 2 more minutes.

2   Reduce the heat and add the shrimp. Simmer for about 5 minutes, just long enough to make them hot. Do not overcook them or they will become rubbery. Serve immediately, garnished with fennel or cilantro sprigs.

¼ cup vegetable oil

2 tablespoons white cumin seeds

1 teaspoon ground turmeric

1 onion, finely chopped

¼ green pepper, chopped

2 tomatoes, skinned and chopped

1–2 green chiles, finely chopped

1½ lb. peeled shrimp

salt

fennel or cilantro sprigs, to garnish

Serves 4
Preparation time: 10 minutes
Cooking time: about 12 minutes

■ Cumin goes well with fish, vegetables, legumes, and grains. Its delicate but permeating flavor also blends well with ground coriander or cilantro.

1½ lb. raw tiger shrimp, peeled and deveined

a 14-oz. can coconut milk

1 tablespoon Thai fish sauce

1 tablespoon light soy sauce

2 garlic cloves, crushed

1-inch piece fresh ginger, grated

1 tablespoon ground coriander

2 teaspoons ground cumin

1 bunch cilantro, chopped

2 red chiles, seeded and sliced

2 teaspoons sugar

2 lemon grass stalks, finely sliced

egg noodles, to serve

To Garnish:

chopped cilantro

chopped red chile

Serves 4
Preparation time: 5–10 minutes
Cooking time: 10–12 minutes

1 Place the shrimp in a shallow, ovenproof dish and set aside. Put all the other ingredients, except the noodles, into a food processor or blender and purée until fairly smooth. Pour the sauce over the shrimp and roast in a preheated oven, 400°F, for 7 minutes, or until the shrimp turn pink and are just cooked through. Remove the shrimp with a slotted spoon, and set aside.

2 Pour the sauce into a small pan and heat for 3–5 minutes to reduce it slightly. Pour the sauce over the shrimp.

3 Serve the shrimp on a bed of egg noodles, garnished with the chopped cilantro and chile.

roasted thai-style shrimp

■ Fish sauce, also known as nam pla, is used in Thai cooking in much the same way as the Chinese use soy sauce. It is available at most large supermarkets and Asian grocery stores.

1 tablespoon oil

1 large onion, chopped

1 garlic clove, crushed

2 celery stalks, thinly sliced

1 cup peeled, seeded, and chopped tomatoes

1 green bell pepper, cored, seeded, and finely chopped

¼ cup dry white wine

1 tablespoon tomato paste

1 lb. peeled, cooked shrimp

2–4 drops Tabasco sauce

1 teaspoon Worcestershire sauce

1 tablespoon chopped parsley

salt and pepper

To Garnish:

lemon twists

celery leaves (optional)

To Serve:

rice or pasta

green salad

Serves 6
Preparation time: 10 minutes
Cooking time: 35–40 minutes

1   Heat the oil in a pan, add the onion and garlic, and fry until lightly browned. Add the celery and cook for 2 minutes.

2   Add the tomatoes and green pepper, and season to taste with salt and pepper. Stir in the wine and tomato paste. Bring to a boil and simmer, uncovered, for 20 minutes.

3   Stir in the shrimp, Tabasco and Worcestershire sauces. Simmer for 5 minutes, then stir in the parsley. Serve immediately, garnished with lemon twists and celery leaves, if you like. Serve with rice or pasta and a green salad.

creole shrimp

spicy baked fish

1 Wash and dry the fish and place in a large dish. Sprinkle with the lime juice and season inside and out with salt and pepper. Leave in a cool place for about 1 hour to marinate.

2 To make the stuffing, put the breadcrumbs into a bowl and mix in the melted butter. Stir in all the remaining stuffing ingredients. Mix well, cover, and set aside.

3 To make the topping, heat the oil in a frying pan and add the onion and garlic. Fry gently until the onion is softened. Add the chile and continue cooking for 2–3 minutes, then stir in the cilantro and stock.

4 Remove the fillets from the marinade and sandwich together with the stuffing. Fasten with wooden toothpicks. Pour over them the oil and any remaining marinade, and scatter the topping mix over the fish. Bake in a preheated oven, 350°F, for 20 minutes. Serve garnished with fried onion rings.

3 lb. sea bass or bream, cleaned, scaled, and filleted

juice of 2 limes

6 tablespoons olive oil

salt and pepper

deep-fried onion rings, to garnish

Stuffing:

4 cups fresh breadcrumbs

½ stick (¼ cup) butter, melted

1 tablespoon finely chopped chives

1 teaspoon finely chopped cilantro

1 small green bell pepper, cored, seeded, and finely chopped

½ onion, grated

grated zest and juice of 1 lime

pinch of grated nutmeg

Topping:

2 tablespoons oil

1 small onion, chopped

1 garlic clove, crushed

1 red chile, seeded and chopped

1 tablespoon chopped cilantro

¼ cup fish stock

Serves 4

Preparation time: 25 minutes plus marinating

Cooking time: 30 minutes

spiced fish cakes

1 Put the skim milk and bay leaf into a pan. Add the fish and poach for 10 minutes, turning once. Leave to cool slightly, then drain and chop the fish, reserving the milk.

2 Meanwhile, make the mint and yogurt sauce. Put the yogurt into a small bowl and beat in the scallions, mint, and lemon juice. Cover with plastic wrap and chill in the refrigerator until ready to serve.

3 Melt the butter in a pan, add the onion and green pepper, and cook over medium heat for 3 minutes, stirring once or twice. Stir in the ground red pepper and cook for 1 minute. Stir in the flour. Pour in the reserved milk, stirring constantly until the sauce boils. Simmer for 3 minutes. Beat the sauce thoroughly. Remove the pan from the heat, beat in the fish, and season with salt. Beat in half of the egg. Leave to cool, then shape into 8 flat cakes.

4 Combine the breadcrumbs and peanuts. In another bowl, beat the remaining egg with the milk. Dip the fish cakes into the egg mixture and then into the breadcrumb mixture to coat. Heat the oil in a nonstick frying pan and fry the cakes for about 3–4 minutes on each side.

5 Spoon a little of the sauce onto each plate and place the fish cakes on top, garnished with the finely chopped scallions. Serve the remaining sauce separately.

1¼ cups skim milk

1 bay leaf

1 lb. pollock or other white fish fillets, skinned

2 tablespoons butter

1 small onion, finely chopped

1 green bell pepper, cored, seeded, and finely chopped

½ teaspoon ground red pepper, or to taste

½ cup whole-wheat flour

1 egg, beaten

¼ cup whole-wheat breadcrumbs

½ cup peanuts, crushed or finely chopped

1 tablespoon milk

2 tablespoons vegetable oil

salt

finely chopped scallions, to garnish

Mint & Yogurt Sauce:

⅔ cup plain yogurt, chilled

3 scallions, finely chopped

2 tablespoons chopped mint

1 teaspoon lemon juice

Serves 4
Preparation time: 25 minutes plus cooling
Cooking time: about 35 minutes

curried chicken salad ●

gado gado with chicken ●

kashmiri chicken ●

chicken jalfrezi ●

trinidadian pilau ●

grilled chicken creole ●

phuket chicken curry ●

deviled chicken ●

spicy pot roast chicken ●

spiced chicken wings & pepper dip ●

red hot turkey sandwich ●

poultry with gusto

curried chicken salad

1 Skin the chicken and remove all the meat from the carcass. Cut the meat into bite-size pieces and place in a bowl with the grapes. Season to taste with salt and pepper. Tear the salad leaves into bite-size pieces and arrange to form a bed on a serving platter or on individual plates.

2 Mix together all the dressing ingredients in a small bowl, adding just enough cold water to give a thick pouring consistency.

3 Add the dressing to the chicken mixture and toss gently until combined. Pile the mixture onto the salad leaves and garnish with a few cilantro sprigs.

■ Chicken salad recipes are great ways of using up leftover cooked chicken.

1 small whole cooked chicken, about 2½ lb.

1¼ cups seedless grapes, cut in half

about ½ lb. mixed salad greens (e.g., romaine, red oak leaf, mâche, arugula, frisé)

salt and pepper

cilantro sprigs, to garnish

Dressing:

6 tablespoons mayonnaise

1 tablespoon medium-hot curry paste

1–2 tablespoons mango chutney

Serves 4

Preparation time: 20 minutes

---

gado gado with chicken

1 Bring a large pot of water to a boil, add the carrot, celery, and leek matchsticks, and blanch for 1–2 minutes. Drain in a colander, rinse under cold running water, then drain again thoroughly. Transfer to a bowl.

2 Cut the snow peas in half diagonally. Using a teaspoon, scoop out the seeds from the cucumber, and cut the flesh into slices. Add the snow peas, cucumber, and bean sprouts to the bowl. Season with salt and pepper. Gently toss together all the vegetables.

3 Arrange the bok choy leaves on a serving platter or individual plates, and top with the shredded chicken and the vegetable mixture. Spoon the dressing over it. Garnish with chopped cilantro.

■ Vegetarians can omit the chicken from this Indonesian salad or replace it with cubed tofu fried in a little oil until golden brown all over.

½ lb. carrots, cut into matchsticks (around 2 cups)

6 oz. celery, cut into matchsticks (around 1½ cups)

6 oz. leeks, cut into matchsticks (around 1½ cups)

4 oz. (around a handful) snow peas

½ cucumber, peeled and cut in half lengthwise

3 cups bean sprouts

6 oz. (around 4–5 small bunches) baby bok choy

2 cooked chicken breasts, skinned and shredded

1 recipe Spicy Peanut Dressing (see page 8)

salt and pepper

chopped cilantro, to garnish

Serves 4
Preparation time: 30 minutes
Cooking time: 1–2 minutes

44

kashmiri chicken

1 Melt the ghee or butter in a wok. Add the onions, peppercorns, cardamom, and cinnamon, and fry for about 8–10 minutes, stirring occasionally, until the onions are golden. Add the ginger, garlic, ground red pepper, paprika, and salt, and fry for 2 minutes, stirring occasionally.

2 Add the chicken pieces and fry until they are evenly browned. Gradually add the yogurt, stirring constantly. Cover and cook for about 30 minutes, or until the chicken is done. Garnish with lime wedges and parsley, and serve with naan bread.

■ Ghee is clarified butter (originally from northern India), from which all the milky solids have been removed, and can be heated to a higher point without burning than unclarified butter can. It is available at Indian grocery stores and markets, and keeps well.

¼ cup ghee or butter

3 large onions, thinly sliced

10 peppercorns

10 cardamom pods

2-inch piece cinnamon stick

2-inch piece fresh ginger, chopped

2 garlic cloves, finely chopped

1 teaspoon ground red pepper

2 teaspoons paprika

3 lb. chicken pieces, skinned

1 cup plain yogurt

salt

naan bread, to serve

To Garnish:

lime wedges

chopped parsley

Serves 4–6	
Preparation time: 10 minutes	
Cooking time: about 45 minutes	

1 Heat the oil in a large, flameproof casserole or cast-iron pan, add the onion, ginger, and garlic, and fry over medium-low heat, stirring frequently, for 5 minutes, until softened but not colored. Add the chiles, garam masala, and ground coriander, and fry, stirring constantly, for 2–3 minutes to release the aroma of the spices. Add the tomatoes, tomato paste, lemon juice, sugar, and ½ teaspoon salt. Stir well to mix, then pour in the stock and bring to a boil over a moderate heat, stirring all the time. Simmer for about 15 minutes, until thickened and reduced.

2 Add the chicken, cover, and simmer over medium-low heat, stirring occasionally, for 30 minutes.

3 Add the chopped green pepper and cilantro and simmer for a further 10 minutes, or until the chicken is tender when pierced with a fork. Taste for seasoning and serve hot, with boiled rice or chapatis and a selection of raitas and chutneys.

2 tablespoons vegetable oil

1 onion, finely chopped

2-inch piece fresh ginger, peeled and crushed

1 garlic clove, crushed

2 small red chiles, very finely chopped

2 teaspoons garam masala

2 teaspoons ground coriander

6 ripe tomatoes, peeled, seeded, and roughly chopped

1 tablespoon tomato paste

2 teaspoons lemon juice

¼ teaspoon sugar

2 cups chicken stock

2 lb. boneless, skinless chicken thighs, cut into bite-size pieces

1 large green bell pepper, cored, seeded, and chopped

2 tablespoons chopped cilantro

salt

To Serve:

boiled rice or chapatis

selection of raitas and chutneys

Serves 4–6
Preparation time: 20 minutes
Cooking time: about 1 hour

chicken jalfrezi

trinidadian pilau

4 lb. chicken, cut into pieces

3 tablespoons peanut oil

1 tablespoon butter

1 onion, finely chopped

2 garlic cloves, crushed

1 red bell pepper, cored, seeded, and chopped

1 red chile pepper, seeded and finely chopped

2 cups long-grain rice

2 tomatoes, peeled and chopped

1 quart chicken stock

a few saffron threads

thyme sprig

Seasoning Mixture:

1 garlic clove

2 allspice berries

1 teaspoon dried mixed herbs

salt and pepper

To Garnish:

½ cup chopped roasted peanuts

chopped red chile

Serves 6

Preparation time: 10 minutes plus marinating

Cooking time: 40 minutes

---

1 Put the ingredients for the seasoning mixture in a mortar and pound well with a pestle until the garlic and allspice berries are crushed and blended with the salt, pepper, and herbs. Rub the seasoning mixture all over the chicken pieces, cover, and leave in the refrigerator for several hours or overnight.

2 Heat the oil and butter in a large frying pan and add the chicken pieces. Fry over medium heat, turning several times, until they are golden brown all over, then remove from the pan and keep warm.

3 Add the onion, garlic, red pepper, and chile to the pan, and fry over medium-low heat until softened but not browned. Add the rice and turn it in the oil until all the grains are coated. Stir in the tomatoes, stock, saffron, and thyme. Return the chicken pieces to the pan, cover, and simmer for about 20 minutes, or until the rice is tender and has absorbed all the liquid and the chicken is cooked. Keep checking the pan and stirring the rice to prevent it from sticking, adding more stock or water, if necessary. Serve hot, sprinkled with peanuts and chile.

grilled chicken creole

1. To prepare the seasoning, put the scallions, onion, garlic, chile, herbs, and allspice berries into a bowl. Add the lime juice and olive oil, and stir well.

2. With a sharp knife, slash the chicken breasts 2–3 times on both sides, and season lightly with salt and pepper. Rub the seasoning over both sides of each breast, pressing it into the slashes. Cover and marinate in the refrigerator for 2–3 hours.

3. Put the chicken breasts on a broiler pan and cook under a preheated hot broiler, turning once, until cooked. Take care that the herbs do not burn. Otherwise you could cook them in a preheated oven, 400°F, for about 20 minutes.

4. While the chicken is cooking, make the avocado sauce. Peel, cut in half, and pit the avocado. Mash to a smooth paste and beat in the onion, garlic, and a little cayenne pepper. Add a little lime juice to prevent the sauce from discoloring. Serve the chicken with the sauce and with some rice.

6 boneless, skinless chicken breasts

salt and pepper

Creole Seasoning:

2 scallions, finely chopped

½ red onion, finely chopped

2 garlic cloves, crushed

1 red chile, seeded and finely chopped

3 chives, snipped

few thyme sprigs, chopped

few parsley sprigs, chopped

3 allspice berries, crushed

juice of 1 lime

2 tablespoons olive oil

Avocado Sauce:

1 large ripe avocado

1 tablespoon finely chopped onion

½ garlic clove, crushed

cayenne pepper, to taste

lime juice

Serves 6

Preparation time: 20 minutes plus marinating

Cooking time: 15–20 minutes

3 tablespoons vegetable oil

4 garlic cloves, crushed

3 shallots, chopped

3 lemon grass stalks, very finely chopped

6 kaffir lime leaves, shredded

3 tablespoons ready-made green curry paste

1 tablespoon Thai fish sauce

2 teaspoons palm sugar or soft brown sugar

1 cup chicken stock

8 large chicken drumsticks

To Garnish:

1 red chile, sliced

kaffir lime leaves (optional)

lemon grass stalks

1 Heat the oil in a large flameproof casserole or cast-iron pan, add the garlic and shallots, and fry over a gentle heat, stirring constantly, for 3 minutes, or until just softened.

2 Add the lemon grass, lime leaves, curry paste, fish sauce, and sugar to the pan. Fry for 1 minute, then add the stock and chicken drumsticks, and bring the curry to a boil. Reduce the heat, cover, and simmer gently, stirring occasionally, for 40–45 minutes, until the chicken is tender and cooked through.

3 Season to taste with salt and pepper, and serve the curry garnished with chile slices, lime leaves, if using, and lemon grass stalks. Serve with noodles or rice.

Serves 4	
Preparation time: 15 minutes	
Cooking time: about 1 hour	

phuket chicken curry

deviled chicken

1 To prepare the chicken, first remove the wings at the first joint, then lay the chicken upside down. Make a lengthwise cut alongside the backbone and open up the chicken. Cut along the other side of the backbone to remove it completely. Remove the shoulder bones from each side. Finally, carefully remove the breastbone, taking care not to pierce through the chicken skin. Make 2 incisions along each leg, one along the thighbone and one along the leg bone, to ensure that both the breasts and legs will be cooked in the same amount of time. Cut a hole in the skin between the point of the breast and the thigh, and push the tip of the drumstick through to secure the leg. Trim any fat and neaten it up.

2 Combine the oil, mustards, Worcestershire sauce, vinegar, onion, honey, Tabasco sauce, garlic, and salt and pepper to taste. Brush both sides of the chicken with half the sauce and place it in a roasting pan, skin side up. Cook in a preheated oven, 350°F, for about 45 minutes, or until the thigh juices run clear when pierced.

3 Transfer the chicken, skin side up, to a broiler pan and brush the skin with the remaining sauce. Broil for 2–3 minutes or until crisp and brown.

4 To serve, cut in half and garnish with the watercress.

one 3-lb. chicken

3 tablespoons vegetable oil

1 tablespoon English mustard powder

1 tablespoon Dijon mustard

1 teaspoon Worcestershire sauce

1 teaspoon white wine vinegar

1 teaspoon grated onion

1 teaspoon clear honey

½–1 teaspoon Tabasco sauce

1 garlic clove, finely chopped

salt and pepper

1 bunch watercress, to garnish

Serves 2

Preparation time: 15–20 minutes

Cooking time: about 50 minutes

spicy pot roast chicken

1 Heat the butter and oil in a flameproof casserole or chicken fryer, and fry the onions until brown. Add the garlic and ginger and fry for 1 minute. Then add the garam masala and coriander and fry for a further minute. Stir in the tomatoes and chiles. Season to taste with salt and pepper and fry for 2–3 minutes. Place the chicken in the pan and seal all over, basting thoroughly with the mixture.

2 Cover the casserole and place in a preheated oven, 350°F, for about 1–1¼ hours, until the chicken is tender, basting once or twice during the cooking. Remove the lid for the last 20 minutes to brown.

3 Garnish with cilantro sprigs and serve the sauce separately.

½ stick (¼ cup) butter

¼ cup oil

2 large onions, sliced

2 garlic cloves, crushed

2 oz. piece fresh ginger, finely chopped

1 tablespoon garam masala

1 tablespoon ground coriander

8 tomatoes, peeled and chopped (see page 24)

2 green chiles, seeded and chopped

one 3½-lb. chicken

salt and pepper

cilantro sprigs, to garnish

Serves 4
Preparation time: 15 minutes
Cooking time: 1½ hours

1 Put all the marinade ingredients into a food processor or blender, and purée until very smooth. Place the chicken in a bowl, pour the marinade over it, and toss well. Cover and leave to marinate for 1–2 hours.

2 To make the dip, put the yellow peppers under a preheated broiler for about 10 minutes, turning them until well charred and blistered. Put them into a plastic bag and leave until cool, then peel off the skins and discard the seeds. Put the flesh into a food processor or blender along with the yogurt, and purée until smooth. Pour into a bowl, season with the soy sauce and pepper to taste, then stir in the cilantro. Set aside.

3 Drain the chicken and cook under a preheated hot broiler for 4–5 minutes on each side, basting with the remaining marinade. Serve with the yellow pepper dip.

8 large chicken wings

salt and pepper

Marinade:

1 garlic clove

2-inch piece fresh ginger, roughly chopped

juice and finely grated zest of 1 lemon

2 tablespoons light soy sauce

2 tablespoons peanut oil

2 teaspoons ground cinnamon

1 teaspoon ground turmeric

2 tablespoons honey

Yellow Pepper Dip:

2 yellow bell peppers

¼ cup plain yogurt

1 tablespoon dark soy sauce

1 tablespoon chopped cilantro

Serves 2–4
Preparation time: 30 minutes plus marinating
Cooking time: 8–10 minutes

spiced chicken wings & pepper dip

red hot turkey sandwich

1. To make the mayonnaise, whisk the egg yolks and vinegar until slightly thickened. Continue to whisk, adding the sunflower oil in a thin steady stream until the mixture forms a thick creamy mayonnaise. Cover and set aside. Place the garlic, pine nuts, and Parmesan in a food processor or blender and purée until smooth. Add the sun-dried tomato halves and chiles and purée until smooth. With the motor running, gradually add 3 tablespoons of the oil from the tomatoes. Spoon the mixture into a bowl and stir in the mayonnaise. Cover and set aside.

2. Place the turkey in a single layer in a shallow dish. Mix the olive oil and orange juice in a cup, and pour this mixture over the turkey, and turn to coat. Cover and marinate for about 30–60 minutes.

3. Drain the turkey, reserving the marinade, then cook the cutlets under a preheated hot broiler for 3–4 minutes on each side, or until tender, basting frequently with the marinade. Remove from the heat, cut into thin strips, and keep hot. Slice the bread in half and toast both halves on the crumb side. Spread each half with some mayonnaise. Divide the artichokes between the bread halves, and add the red onion, arugula, and sliced hot turkey. Sprinkle with salt and pepper to taste, and serve.

four ¼-lb. turkey cutlets

¼ cup olive oil

3 tablespoons orange juice

1 large loaf focaccia or olive bread

4 artichoke hearts in oil, drained and sliced

1 red onion, thinly sliced into rings

4 oz. (around 2 large handfuls) arugula

salt and pepper

Red Hot Mayonnaise:

2 egg yolks

1 tablespoon white wine vinegar

a scant cup sunflower oil

2 garlic cloves, crushed

¼ cup pine nuts

¼ cup grated Parmesan cheese

8 sun-dried tomato halves in oil

2 red chiles, peeled (see page 28) and seeded

Serves 4

Preparation time: 20 minutes plus marinating

Cooking time: 6–8 minutes

meat-stuffed tortillas ●

chili stir-fry with steak ●

chile con carne ●

mexican beef with lime rice ●

lamb casserole with roasted garlic & chile ●

chorizo kebabs with celeriac & garlic purée ●

chile pork ●

griddled sausages & mustard mash ●

sweet & spicy pork ●

meat with a kick

meat-stuffed tortillas

1 Put the ground pork and beef into a large frying pan and cook in their own fat until browned and crumbly, breaking up the meat with a wooden spoon. Add the oil, onion, and garlic, and cook until soft. Stir in the chili powder, cumin, oregano, and salt, then the vinegar and stock. Simmer for 10 minutes, or until the liquid has evaporated. Remove from the heat and leave to cool.

2 Spread some of the salsa cruda over each tortilla and put about 2 tablespoons of the meat filling down the center of each one. Fold over, secure with a cocktail stick, and arrange in a casserole.

3 Pour the remaining salsa cruda over the tortillas and sprinkle the grated Cheddar cheese over them. Bake in a preheated oven, 350°F, for 20–30 minutes, or until golden brown. Remove the tortillas from the dish and garnish with the radish or olive slices, chili flakes, and red chile slices.

1 lb. ground pork

1 lb. ground beef

1 tablespoon olive oil

1 large onion, finely chopped

2 garlic cloves, crushed

1 tablespoon chili powder

½ teaspoon ground cumin

2 teaspoons dried oregano

pinch of salt

¼ cup vinegar

1 cup beef stock

2 cups Salsa Cruda (see page 9)

12 ready-made corn or flour tortillas

¾ cup grated Cheddar cheese

To Garnish:

sliced radishes or olives

dried chili flakes

1 red chile, seeded and finely sliced

Serves 4
Preparation time: 20 minutes
Cooking time: 30–40 minutes

chili stir-fry with steak

1 Heat the oil in a wok. Add the diced steak, a little at a time, and stir-fry until sealed all over. Add the garlic and stir-fry for about 2 minutes, until it has blended with the meat; add the ginger and stir-fry for 2 minutes more. Sprinkle in all the spices, and stir-fry until the pieces of meat are coated in them. The meat should be dry without sticking to the pan. Strain the tomatoes and use the juice to moisten the meat, if necessary.

2 Add the onion, a tablespoon at a time, allowing each spoonful to be absorbed by the meat before adding the next. Stir-fry for another 3–4 minutes. By now the meat should have cooked for about 20 minutes and will be half cooked. Add the remaining tomato juice, the tomatoes, chiles, and chili powder to taste. Season with salt to taste, cover, and continue to cook for about 20 minutes, or until the meat is tender. Serve immediately.

¼ cup vegetable oil

1½ lb. lean sirloin steak, diced

2–3 garlic cloves, finely chopped

2-inch piece fresh ginger, finely chopped

2 teaspoons coriander seeds, toasted and ground

1 teaspoon cumin seeds, toasted and ground

½ teaspoon fennel seeds, toasted and ground

½ teaspoon fenugreek seeds, toasted and ground

1 teaspoon ground turmeric

2 teaspoons paprika

a 14-oz. can tomatoes

1 large onion, very finely chopped

2–6 fresh green chiles, chopped

2–4 teaspoons chili powder

salt

Serves 4

Preparation time: 30 minutes

Cooking time: about 40 minutes

chile con carne

1 Heat the oil in a pan, add the onions, red pepper, and garlic, and fry gently until soft. Add the meat and fry until just colored.

2 Blend in the stock and add the chili powder, beans, tomatoes, cumin, and salt and pepper to taste. Bring to a boil, cover, lower the heat, and simmer gently for 50–60 minutes, stirring occasionally.

3 Meanwhile, boil the rice for 10 minutes, or according to the package instructions, in plenty of lightly salted boiling water, until tender. Drain well. Serve the chile con carne on a bed of rice, with the sour cream, chile seeds, and grated Cheddar. Garnish with the scallion.

■ Since the seeds are the hottest part of a chile, only use them as a garnish if you and your guests have a taste for quite fiery food.

2 tablespoons oil

3 onions, chopped

1 red pepper, cored, seeded, and diced

2 garlic cloves, crushed

1 lb. lean ground beef

2 cups beef stock

1 teaspoon chili powder

2 cups cooked red kidney beans

a 14-oz. can chopped tomatoes

½ teaspoon ground cumin

1⅓ cups long-grain rice

salt and pepper

finely chopped scallion, to garnish

To Serve:

sour cream

chile seeds (optional)

grated Cheddar cheese

Serves 4
Preparation time: 15 minutes
Cooking time: 1¼ hours

2 tablespoons vegetable oil

1 lb. lean ground beef

1 onion, finely chopped

1 red or green bell pepper, cored, seeded, and diced

2 garlic cloves, finely chopped

1 tablespoon tomato paste

½ teaspoon chili powder, or to taste

1 teaspoon cumin seeds, toasted

¾ cup frozen corn kernels

1 cup cooked or canned red kidney beans

2 cups vegetable stock

1⅓ cups long-grain rice

1¼ cups water

juice of 2 limes

3 tablespoons finely chopped cilantro

salt and pepper

½ green chile, seeded and finely sliced, to garnish

1 Heat the oil in a heavy pan, add the beef and fry, stirring frequently, until browned. Stir in the onion, red or green pepper, and garlic, and fry until just soft. Add the tomato paste, chili powder, cumin, corn, beans, and vegetable stock, and season to taste with salt and pepper. Bring to a boil, then simmer for 45 minutes, stirring occasionally.

2 When the beef has simmered for about 25 minutes, put the rice, water, lime juice, and ½ teaspoon of salt into another pan. Bring to a boil and stir once. Cover and simmer for 15 minutes, or according to the package instructions.

3 Lightly fluff up the rice with a fork and stir in the chopped cilantro. Serve the beef garnished with the chile strips and accompanied by a portion of lime rice.

Serves 4
Preparation time: 10 minutes
Cooking time: 1 hour

mexican beef with lime rice

62

lamb casserole with roasted garlic & chile

1 Put the chiles and garlic on a baking sheet and roast in a preheated oven, 425°F, for about 15–20 minutes. Cool slightly, then peel off the skins, and remove the seeds from the chiles. Put the chile and garlic flesh into a small bowl with the coriander and cumin seeds, and mash to a paste.

2 Heat 1 tablespoon of the oil in a heavy pan, add the lamb cubes and brown. Remove the lamb and set aside. Heat the remaining oil in the pan and gently fry the onion for 5 minutes. Add the chile-garlic paste, and stir-fry for another minute.

3 Return the lamb to the pan and add the rice, chickpeas, tomatoes, eggplant, beans, stock, and season to taste. Bring to a boil, then cover and simmer gently for 1–1½ hours, or until tender. Stir in the cilantro. Serve with the yogurt, and garnish each serving with a red chile.

2 large red or green chiles

2 large garlic cloves, unpeeled

1 teaspoon coriander seeds, toasted and crushed

1 teaspoon cumin seeds, toasted and crushed

3 tablespoons vegetable oil

1½ lb. boneless lamb, cubed

1 onion, chopped

2⅔ cups cooked long-grain brown rice

¾ cup cooked chickpeas

a 14-oz. can chopped tomatoes

1 large eggplant, diced

½ cup chopped green beans

2 cups vegetable stock

3 tablespoons finely chopped cilantro

salt and pepper

red chiles, to garnish

plain yogurt, to serve

Serves 4

Preparation time: 20 minutes

Cooking time: about 1½–2 hours

1 Place the celeriac in a pot. Cover with lightly salted cold water and bring to a boil. Cover the pot, lower the heat, and simmer gently for 15–20 minutes, until tender. Drain and add the garlic. Add the butter, season to taste with salt and pepper, and mash well. Transfer the purée to a warmed bowl.

2 Heat a griddle or frying pan. Cut each onion into 8 wedges, cutting almost, but not all the way through, so they remain attached at the root end. Place the onion wedges on the griddle and cook for about 4 minutes on each side, or until they are charred. If they are charring too much, reduce the heat.

3 Meanwhile, thread the lengths of sausage onto 4 long metal skewers, alternating with sage leaves. Cook under a preheated hot broiler for 8–10 minutes, turning occasionally, until slightly crisp and heated through.

4 Serve the griddled onions and sausage kebabs with the celeriac purée.

1½ lb. celeriac, peeled and cut into 1-inch cubes

8 large garlic cloves, roasted (see page 62)

2 tablespoons butter

4 red onions, unpeeled

4 large chorizo or merguez sausages, cut into 1-inch lengths

sage leaves stripped from the stalks of 1 bunch of sage

salt and pepper

Serves 4	
Preparation time: 30 minutes	
Cooking time: 20 minutes	

chorizo kebabs with celeriac & garlic purée

3 tablespoons vegetable oil

¼ lb. ground pork

2 tomatoes, diced

5 teaspoons sugar

5 teaspoons Thai fish sauce

cilantro, to garnish

Chile Paste:

5 small shallots

3 large dried red chiles, soaked for 20 minutes

12 cilantro roots

Salad:

½ cucumber, cut into chunks

1 small lettuce, separated into leaves

cilantro sprigs

Serves 2
Preparation time: 10 minutes
Cooking time: 6–8 minutes

1 To make the chile paste, put the shallots, chiles, and cilantro roots into a food processor or blender and purée, adding a little water if the mixture seems very dry. Or, you could pound them together in a mortar until thoroughly combined.

2 Heat the oil in a wok, add the chile paste, and stir-fry for 30 seconds. Add the pork and tomatoes, and cook, stirring, for 30 seconds, then add the sugar and fish sauce and continue to cook, stirring, for 4–5 minutes.

3 Transfer the pork to a bowl, garnish with cilantro, and serve with the salad on the side.

chile pork

■ This recipe could be served as part of a Thai meal. Serve it with a noodle dish, such as Shrimp & Noodles in Spicy Broth (see page 29) or Chiang mai Noodles (see page 78).

griddled sausages & mustard mash

1 Heat a griddle or frying pan. Put the potatoes into a pot of cold water, bring to a boil, and simmer for 15 minutes.

2 Meanwhile, place the sausages on the griddle and cook for 10 minutes, turning occasionally. Add the onion wedges and cook with the sausages for 6–7 minutes.

3 When the potatoes are cooked, drain them well, and return to the pot. Put the pot over a low heat so that any excess water steams away, without coloring the potatoes. Remove from the heat; peel the potatoes and mash well. Add the butter, mustards, and garlic, and season with salt and pepper, and continue to mash. Taste the potato and add more mustard if you like, then add the parsley and a dash of olive oil, and stir. Serve the mash and sausages with the griddled onion wedges.

■ It is well worth investing in a ridged cast-iron griddle pan. Not only is griddling a quick and easy way of cooking, but it is also a healthy one, and the results look good as well.

8 good-quality sausages

2 onions, cut into wedges, roots left intact

Mustard Mash:

2 lb. potatoes, quartered but unpeeled

¾ stick (⅓ cup) butter

1 tablespoon whole-grain mustard

1 tablespoon prepared English mustard

1 garlic clove, crushed

1 large bunch parsley, chopped

dash of olive oil

sea salt and pepper

Serves 4
Preparation time: 10 minutes
Cooking time: 25 minutes

sweet & spicy pork

1 Cut the tenderloin crosswise into ¾-inch slices, then cut these slices crosswise into 2–3 strips. Mix the sauce ingredients in a glass measuring cup, add cold water up to the 1 cup mark, and mix well.

2 Heat a wok until hot. Add the oil and swirl around the sides of the pan until very hot. Add the scallions, ginger, and garlic, and stir-fry over medium heat for about 1 minute. Add the carrots and stir-fry for 1–2 minutes.

3 Increase the heat to high, add the pork, and stir-fry for about 5 minutes. Pour in the sauce mixture and bring to a boil, stirring all the time, then simmer for about 2 minutes, or until the sauce is thick and reduced. Taste, and add more chile sauce, if you like.

4 Add the bean sprouts and toss vigorously to mix all the ingredients together. Sprinkle with the pomegranate seeds, if using, and serve immediately.

1 pork tenderloin, about ¾ lb.

¼ cup peanut oil

5 scallions, chopped

1-inch piece fresh ginger, finely chopped

2 garlic cloves, finely chopped

3 carrots, thinly sliced

1¾ cups bean sprouts

seeds of 1 pomegranate (optional)

Chile-Soy Sauce:

¼ cup rice wine or sherry

2–3 tablespoons soy sauce

2–3 tablespoons chile sauce

2 tablespoons honey

1 tablespoon tomato paste

2 teaspoons cornstarch

Serves 4

Preparation time: 30 minutes

Cooking time: about 15 minutes

sizzling vegetables

black bean chili

1 Put the beans into a pot with the water and bring to a boil. Boil rapidly for 10 minutes, then reduce the heat, cover the pan, and simmer for 45 minutes.

2 Meanwhile, heat half the oil in a pan and stir-fry the mushrooms for 5 minutes. Remove from the pan and set aside. Add the remaining oil to the pan along with the onion, garlic, potatoes, red or green pepper, and spices, and fry over a moderate heat for 10 minutes.

3 Drain the beans, reserving the liquid. Boil the liquid until reduced to 2 cups. Stir the beans into the pan with the vegetables and add the reduced cooking liquid, tomato purée, and mushrooms. Bring to a boil, cover, and simmer for 30 minutes.

4 Stir in the lime juice, chocolate, and cilantro, and cook for a further 5 minutes. Serve hot, topped with a spoon of avocado salsa, if using.

1 cup dried black beans, soaked overnight and drained

1½ quarts water

¼ cup extra-virgin olive oil

½ lb. (2 heaped cups) small mushrooms, cut in half

1 large onion, chopped

2 garlic cloves, crushed

2 large potatoes, cubed

1 red or green bell pepper, cored, seeded, and diced

2 teaspoons ground coriander

1 teaspoon ground cumin

2 teaspoons hot chili powder

2 cups tomato purée

1 tablespoon lime juice

⅓ cup chopped unsweetened baking chocolate

2 tablespoons finely chopped cilantro

Avocado Salsa (see page 15), to serve (optional)

Serves 8

Preparation time: 20 minutes plus soaking and making the salsa (optional)

Cooking time: 1½ hours

■ Chocolate is a traditional ingredient used in some savory Mexican and Spanish dishes. Use bitter or unsweetened chocolate.

Dressing:

3 tablespoons mayonnaise

½ teaspoon curry powder

½ teaspoon grated nutmeg

½ teaspoon paprika

1 teaspoon English mustard powder

1 tablespoon olive oil

1 tablespoon lemon juice

salt and pepper

Salad:

¼–½ green cabbage or cabbage heart

1 unpeeled eating apple, cored and diced

2 carrots, grated

2 tablespoons diced gherkins

2 teaspoons capers

2 tablespoons chopped parsley

Serves 4
Preparation time: 25–30 minutes

1 First make the dressing. Mix together all of the ingredients in a measuring cup.

2 Shred the cabbage finely by hand, or use a food processor, then put it into a serving bowl. Add the apple and carrots along with the gherkins, capers, and parsley. Pour the dressing over them, and mix thoroughly. Serve immediately.

spiced coleslaw

■ Don't make the coleslaw too far in advance, as the cabbage and other salad ingredients should be served as fresh and crisp as possible.

spicy potatoes

1 Heat the oil in a heavy pan, add the mustard seeds, and fry until they pop; this should only take a few seconds. Add the potatoes and fry for about 5 minutes. Add the spices, lemon juice, sugar, and salt to taste, stir well, and cook for 5 minutes.

2 Add the tomatoes, stir well, then simmer for 5–10 minutes, until the potatoes are tender. Serve garnished with cilantro.

2 tablespoons vegetable oil

½ teaspoon mustard seeds

½ lb. potatoes, cut into small cubes (around 1⅓ cups)

1 teaspoon ground turmeric

1 teaspoon chili powder

2 teaspoons paprika

¼ cup lemon juice

1 teaspoon sugar

½ lb. (around 2 medium) tomatoes, quartered

salt

2 tablespoons chopped cilantro, to garnish

Serves 4
Preparation time: 10 minutes
Cooking time: 20 minutes

■ Turmeric is often regarded as a poor man's saffron—largely because it is so much less expensive. It has a more bitter taste than saffron and is an ingredient in commercial curry powders. Be careful not to spill it as it will stain clothes and work surfaces.

vegetable fajitas

1 Heat the olive oil in a large frying pan and gently sauté the onions and garlic for about 5 minutes, until soft and golden brown.

2 Add the red and green peppers, chiles, and oregano or cilantro, and stir well. Sauté gently for about 10 minutes, until cooked and just tender.

3 Add the mushrooms and cook quickly for 1 minute more, stirring to mix the mushrooms thoroughly with the other vegetables. Season the vegetable mixture with salt and pepper to taste.

4 To serve, spoon the sizzling hot vegetable mixture into the warmed tortillas, and roll up or fold over. Serve hot, garnished with chives.

2 tablespoons olive oil

2 large onions, thinly sliced

2 garlic cloves, crushed

2 red bell peppers, cored, seeded, and thinly sliced

2 green bell peppers, cored, seeded, and thinly sliced

4 green chiles, seeded and thinly sliced

2 teaspoons chopped oregano or cilantro

½ lb. (2 heaped cups) button mushrooms, sliced

salt and pepper

12 warmed tortillas, to serve

chives, to garnish

Serves 4

Preparation time: 15 minutes

Cooking time: 15–20 minutes

2–3 tablespoons vegetable oil

1 small onion, chopped

1 garlic clove, crushed

1-inch piece fresh ginger, grated

1 teaspoon ground red pepper

2 teaspoons ground coriander

½ teaspoon ground turmeric

1 lb. diced mixed vegetables (e.g., potatoes, carrots, rutabaga, peas, beans, cauliflower)

2–3 tomatoes, skinned and chopped (see page 24)

salt

Indian bread, to serve

Serves 4

Preparation time: 15 minutes

Cooking time: 20–30 minutes

1 Heat the oil in a wok or heavy-based pot, and gently fry the onion for 5–10 minutes, or until lightly browned.

2 Add the garlic, ginger, ground red pepper, coriander, turmeric, and a pinch of salt. Fry gently for 2–3 minutes, then add the diced vegetables and stir-fry for a further 2–3 minutes.

3 Add the chopped tomatoes, stir well, and add a little water. Cover and cook for 10–12 minutes, or until the vegetables are tender, adding a little more water, if necessary, to prevent the vegetables from sticking to the base of the wok. Serve immediately with Indian bread.

spicy indian vegetables

spicy zucchini

1 Heat the ghee or butter in a heavy frying pan, add the onion, and fry for 5 minutes, stirring occasionally, until softened.

2 Add the asafetida, if using, then add the potatoes and fry for 2–3 minutes.

3 Stir in the sliced zucchini, the ground red pepper, turmeric, coriander, and salt. Add the water, cover the pan, and cook gently for 8–10 minutes, until the potatoes are tender. Sprinkle with the garam masala and garnish with chopped cilantro. Serve immediately with Indian bread.

2 tablespoons ghee or butter

1 small onion, chopped

pinch of asafetida (optional)

2 small potatoes, quartered

12 oz. zucchini, sliced (around 2½ generous cups)

½ teaspoon ground red pepper

½ teaspoon ground turmeric

1 teaspoon ground coriander

½ teaspoon salt

⅔ cup water

½ teaspoon garam masala

chopped cilantro, to garnish

Indian bread, to serve

Serves 4
Preparation time: 10 minutes
Cooking time: about 15 minutes

½ cup vegetable oil

2 teaspoons cumin seeds

1 large onion, chopped

a 13-oz. can chopped tomatoes

1 tablespoon ground coriander

1 teaspoon ground red pepper

1 teaspoon sugar

1 teaspoon salt

two 14-oz. cans red kidney beans, drained and rinsed

cilantro, to garnish

To Serve:

boiled rice

sour cream

Serves 4–6
Preparation time: 15 minutes
Cooking time: 30–35 minutes

1 Heat the oil in a wok or frying pan, add the cumin seeds and chopped onion, and fry until the onion is lightly browned. Stir in the tomatoes and fry for a few seconds, then add the ground coriander, ground red pepper, sugar, and salt, and stir well. Lower the heat, and cook for about 5–7 minutes.

2 Add the drained kidney beans, stir carefully but thoroughly, and cook for 10–15 minutes. Garnish with cilantro and serve with rice and a dollop of sour cream.

kidney bean curry

chiang mai noodles

1 Cook the noodles in boiling water for 5–6 minutes. Drain, rinse in cold water to stop further cooking, and drain again.

2 Heat the oil in a wok, add the garlic, and stir-fry until golden. Add the curry paste and chiles and mix thoroughly. Pour in the coconut milk, stirring continuously, then bring to a boil and cook until the liquid thickens a little.

3 Add the stock, turmeric, curry powder, fish or soy sauce, and sugar, and return to a boil. Lower the heat and add the celery, shallot, red pepper, mushrooms, and peanuts. Bring back to a boil, then remove from the heat.

4 To serve, put the noodles into a large serving bowl, pour the sauce over them, and sprinkle with lime juice to taste.

■ To prepare the nuts, dry-fry unroasted peanuts in a preheated wok, stirring, until they turn golden. Remove from the heat. When cooled, put them in a plastic bag and crush with a rolling pin. Store for up to 1 month in an airtight container in the refrigerator.

6 oz. dried egg noodles

1 tablespoon peanut oil

2 garlic cloves, finely chopped

2 tablespoons Thai Red Curry Paste (see page 8)

¼ teaspoon crushed dried chiles

1 cup coconut milk

2 cups vegetable stock

¼ teaspoon ground turmeric

1½ teaspoons curry powder

2 tablespoons Thai fish sauce or soy sauce

1 tablespoon palm sugar or light brown sugar

⅓ cup chopped celery

1 medium shallot, finely sliced

a quarter of a red bell pepper, chopped

1 cup dried shiitake mushrooms, soaked, drained, and sliced

1 tablespoon crushed roasted peanuts (see below, left)

2 tablespoons lime juice, to serve

Serves 4 as part of a Thai meal

Preparation time: 30 minutes plus soaking

Cooking time: 15 minutes

vegetable biryani

1 Bring a large pot of salted water to a rolling boil, add the basmati rice, and return to a simmer. Cook gently for 5 minutes. Drain, rinse under cold water, and drain again. Spread the rice on a large baking sheet and set aside to dry.

2 Heat 2 tablespoons of the oil in a frying pan, add half the onion and fry over a moderate heat for 10 minutes, until very crisp and golden. Remove and drain on paper towels. Set aside for garnishing.

3 Add the rest of the oil to the pan, and fry the remaining onion, with the garlic and ginger, for 5 minutes. Add the sweet potato, carrots, and spices, and fry for a further 10 minutes, until light golden. Add the stock and tomatoes, and bring to a boil. Cover the pan and simmer gently for 20 minutes. Add the cauliflower and peas, and cook for 8–10 minutes, until all the vegetables are tender.

4 Stir in the rice, cashew nuts, and cilantro. Cook, stirring, for 3 minutes, then cover and remove from the heat. Leave to stand for 5 minutes, then serve garnished with the crispy onions and egg quarters.

1⅓ cups basmati rice, rinsed

¼ cup plus 2 tablespoons vegetable oil

2 large onions, thinly sliced

2 garlic cloves, crushed

2 teaspoons grated fresh ginger

1½ cups diced sweet potato

2 large carrots, diced

1 tablespoon curry paste

2 teaspoons ground turmeric

1 teaspoon ground cinnamon

1 teaspoon ground red pepper

1¼ cups vegetable stock

4 ripe tomatoes, peeled, seeded, and diced (see page 24)

6 oz. cauliflower florets (around ¾ cup)

1 cup frozen peas, thawed

½ cup cashew nuts, toasted

2 tablespoons chopped cilantro

salt

2 hard-boiled eggs, quartered, to serve

Serves 4

Preparation time: 25 minutes

Cooking time: about 1 hour

1   Heat the oil for deep-frying to 350–375°F, or until a cube of bread browns in 30 seconds. Deep-fry the tofu cubes in batches for about 1 minute, or until they are crisp and golden. Remove with a slotted spoon, drain thoroughly on paper towels, and set aside.

2   Heat the vegetable oil in a heavy-based pan, add the shallots, chiles, garlic, ginger, and lemon grass, and fry over a gentle heat, stirring frequently, for 5 minutes, or until just softened.

3   Add the ground spices and shrimp paste, and fry for a further minute. Stir in the stock and coconut milk, and bring to a boil. Add the potatoes, reduce the heat, and cook for 6 minutes. Add the beans and cook for 8 minutes.

4   Stir in the cabbage, bean sprouts, and rice vermicelli, and season to taste with salt. Cook gently for 3 minutes. Stir in the fried tofu and serve immediately.

oil, for deep-frying

4 squares pressed bean curd (tofu), cut into 1-inch cubes

2 tablespoons vegetable oil

4 shallots, sliced

2 green chiles, seeded and sliced

3 garlic cloves, chopped

1 tablespoon finely chopped fresh ginger

1 lemon grass stalk, finely chopped

1 tablespoon ground coriander

1 teaspoon ground cumin

1 teaspoon ground turmeric

1 teaspoon galangal (laos) powder

1 teaspoon ground red pepper

1 teaspoon shrimp paste

2½ cups vegetable stock

1¾ cups coconut milk

1½–1¾ cups diced potatoes

¼ lb. green beans, cut into ½-inch lengths (around ¾ cup)

2 cups finely shredded green cabbage

1½ cups bean sprouts

1 oz. dried rice vermicelli, soaked in boiling water for 5 minutes, then drained

salt

Serves 6	
Preparation time: 20 minutes	
Cooking time: 35 minutes	

vegetable curry

tagliatelle with chile balsamic sauce •

pasta with calabrian sauce •

fettuccine with spicy tomato sauce •

peppery chicken with pasta •

chinese beef cappellini •

indian meatballs with tomato curry sauce •

penne all'arrabbiata •

quick focaccia pizza with pepperoni •

chili-topped pizza •

spicy hot pizza •

pasta
& pizza

12 oz. dried tagliatelle

¼ cup olive oil

2 garlic cloves, crushed

2 red chiles, seeded
and chopped

¼ cup balsamic vinegar

2 tablespoons orange juice

3 tablespoons sun-dried tomato
paste

1 bunch scallions, shredded

¼ cup chopped toasted hazelnuts

salt

grated Parmesan cheese,
to serve (optional)

1 Cook the pasta in plenty of lightly salted boiling water for 8–12 minutes, or according to the package instructions, until just tender.

2 Meanwhile, heat the oil in a pan. Add the garlic and chiles and fry for 2 minutes. Reduce the heat and stir in the vinegar, orange juice, red pesto, shredded scallions, and chopped hazelnuts. Season to taste with salt.

3 Drain the tagliatelle and pile it into a warmed bowl. Pour the sauce over it and toss well. Sprinkle with grated Parmesan, if you like.

Serves 4

Preparation time: 10 minutes

Cooking time: 8–12 minutes

tagliatelle with chile balsamic sauce

pasta with calabrian sauce

1 Crush the tomatoes or purée them briefly in a food processor or blender. Coat a pan with olive oil. Add the garlic and chile, and fry gently until the garlic is golden, and crush the chile against the bottom of the pan to release its flavor. Add the tomatoes and the slices of salami, and season to taste with salt. Simmer gently for about 30 minutes, until the sauce thickens and darkens in color.

2 Meanwhile, cook the pasta in lightly salted boiling water for 8–12 minutes, or according to the package instructions, until just tender.

3 Drain the pasta, transfer to a warmed serving dish, and pour the sauce over the top. Serve with Romano cheese shavings and a generous grinding of pepper.

a 20-oz. can tomatoes

olive oil, for frying

2 garlic cloves, each cut into 3–4 pieces

1 chile, seeded

¼ lb. salami, thickly sliced

1 lb. dried shell pasta or other pasta shapes

salt and pepper

Romano cheese shavings, to serve

Serves 4–6
Preparation time: 15 minutes
Cooking time: about 35 minutes

1 Cook the pasta in plenty of lightly salted boiling water for 8–12 minutes, or according to the package instructions, until just tender.

2 Meanwhile, heat the oil in a large frying pan. Add the garlic, ground red pepper and coriander. Fry over medium heat for 1 minute, stirring constantly. Stir in the pepperoni, the tomatoes with their juices, tomato purée, and red wine, and season to taste with salt and pepper. Simmer, uncovered, for about 10 minutes.

3 Drain the pasta and add it to the sauce. Toss and season with more pepper, if you like. Add the basil and toss again to mix. Sprinkle with thyme to garnish. Serve immediately.

12 oz. dried fettuccine

2 tablespoons olive oil

3 garlic cloves, crushed

1 teaspoon ground red pepper

1 teaspoon ground coriander

¼ lb. sliced pepperoni

a 13-oz. can chopped tomatoes

6 tablespoons tomato purée

¼ cup red wine

1 tablespoon basil leaves

salt and pepper

thyme sprigs, to garnish

Serves 4
Preparation time: 10 minutes
Cooking time: 12 minutes

fettuccine with spicy tomato sauce

peppery chicken with pasta

1 In a bowl, mix together the ground red pepper, cayenne, turmeric, and 1 teaspoon of the olive oil. Stir to form a paste. Add the chicken pieces and coat thoroughly in the spice mixture. Cover and set aside for 15 minutes.

2 Meanwhile, heat the remaining olive oil in a large frying pan. Add the onion and fry for 3 minutes, until softened but not colored. Add the tomatoes with the can juices, and the sugar. Strip the basil leaves from the stems. Set some leaves aside for the garnish. Chop the rest finely and add them to the pan. Boil the mixture rapidly for 5 minutes, stirring occasionally to break up the tomatoes.

3 Cook the pasta in plenty of lightly salted boiling water for 8–12 minutes, or according to the package instructions, until just tender.

4 While the pasta is cooking, dry-fry the spicy chicken pieces in a nonstick frying pan for 10 minutes, or until crisp. Add to the sauce. Drain the pasta, drizzle with a little more oil, and season to taste with salt and pepper. Arrange the pasta on a large, warmed serving platter and pour the sauce over it. Serve immediately, garnished with the reserved basil leaves.

■ "Pipe rigate" are small curved elbow-shaped pasta with a ribbed or "rigate" surface.

1 teaspoon ground red pepper

1 teaspoon cayenne pepper

1 teaspoon ground turmeric

1 tablespoon olive oil plus a little extra for drizzling

½ lb. skinless chicken breast, cut into bite-size pieces

1 onion, chopped

a 13-oz. can plum tomatoes

1 teaspoon sugar

1 bunch basil

12 oz. dried pipe rigate or other pasta shapes

salt and pepper

Serves 4

Preparation time: 15 minutes plus marinating

Cooking time: 25–30 minutes

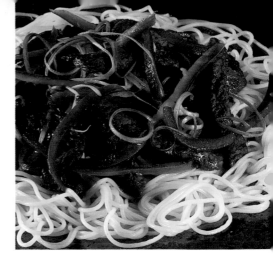

1 Cut the steak into ¼-inch-wide strips. In a bowl, mix together the red peppercorns, ground red pepper, Szechuan pepper, light soy sauce, and sherry. Add the steak strips to the marinade and toss to coat thoroughly.

2 Cook the pasta in plenty of lightly salted boiling water for 8–12 minutes, or according to the package instructions, until just tender.

3 While the pasta is cooking, heat a wok. Add the oil and heat until a blue haze can be seen. Set aside a few of the shredded scallions for the garnish, and add the rest to the wok with the sliced peppers, and stir-fry for 2 minutes. Then add the marinated beef and the marinade, and stir-fry for 5 minutes.

4 Drain the pasta. Place in a large warmed serving bowl and spoon the beef and pepper mixture over the top. Garnish with the reserved shredded scallions and serve immediately.

1 lb. sirloin steak

1 tablespoon crushed red peppercorns

1 tablespoon ground red pepper

1–2 tablespoons Szechuan pepper

3 tablespoons light soy sauce

3 tablespoons dry sherry

12 oz. dried cappellini

2 teaspoons sesame or light vegetable oil

1 bunch scallions, shredded

1 red bell pepper, cored, seeded, and thinly sliced

1 green bell pepper, cored, seeded, and thinly sliced

salt

Serves 4
Preparation time: 10 minutes
Cooking time: 15–20 minutes

chinese beef cappellini

1 onion, grated

1 cup grated Parmesan cheese

1 lb. ground lean lamb

1 tablespoon tomato paste

1 teaspoon chile sauce

1 tablespoon ground coriander

1 tablespoon ground cumin

¼ cup olive oil plus extra
for drizzling

12 oz. dried spaghetti

salt and pepper

Tomato Curry Sauce:

1 tablespoon olive oil

1 onion, finely chopped

2 garlic cloves, crushed

1 tablespoon curry powder

2 tablespoons tomato paste

a 13-oz. can chopped tomatoes

2 teaspoons garam masala

2 tablespoons finely chopped
cilantro

cilantro to garnish

Serves 4
Preparation time: 20 minutes
Cooking time: about 30 minutes

1 To make the meatballs, combine the onion, cheese, lamb, tomato paste, chile sauce, ground coriander, and cumin. Add salt and pepper, and mix thoroughly. With dampened hands, divide the mixture into 28–32 pieces and shape into small balls. Heat the oil in a large frying pan and fry the meatballs in 2 batches for 10 minutes each. Using a slotted spoon, transfer the meatballs to an ovenproof dish. Keep hot.

2 Bring at least 2 quarts of water to a boil in a large pot. Add a dash of oil and a generous pinch of salt. Cook the pasta for 8–12 minutes, or according to the package instructions, until just tender.

3 Meanwhile, make the sauce. Heat the oil in a frying pan, add the onion and garlic, and fry for 3–5 minutes, or until the onion has softened. Stir in the curry powder, tomato paste, and chopped tomatoes. Simmer the sauce, uncovered, for 5–10 minutes, then sprinkle in the garam masala, followed by the chopped cilantro. Stir well.

4 Drain the pasta, pile it in a heated bowl, and drizzle with a little oil. Season to taste with pepper. Pour the sauce over the pasta and toss lightly. Serve with the meatballs and garnish with cilantro.

indian meatballs with tomato curry sauce

■ Ground lamb is available at most butchers and supermarkets, but it often contains quite a lot of fat. For best results, buy a single piece of lean lamb and grind it yourself using a meat grinder or food processor.

1 Purée the tomatoes in a food processor or blender, then set aside until needed.

2 In a large pot, melt the butter over a moderate heat. Add the onion and bacon, and cook, stirring, for 5 minutes. Add the garlic and chiles, then cook, stirring occasionally, for a further 5 minutes, or until the onion is tender. Add the tomatoes, oregano, and thyme, and season to taste with salt and pepper. Cover and simmer for 30 minutes.

3 Meanwhile, cook the pasta in plenty of lightly salted boiling water for 8–12 minutes, or according to the package instructions, until just tender. Drain well.

4 Add the pasta to the sauce and toss gently. Transfer to a warmed serving dish and sprinkle with the Parmesan. Garnish with the parsley and serve immediately.

two 13-oz. cans tomatoes, drained

2 tablespoons butter

1 onion, finely chopped

¼ lb. bacon, diced

2 garlic cloves, finely chopped

1–2 red chiles, finely chopped

1 tablespoon chopped oregano

1 tablespoon chopped thyme

12 oz. dried penne

2 cups grated Parmesan cheese

1 tablespoon chopped parsley, to garnish

salt and pepper

Serves 4
Preparation time: 10–15 minutes
Cooking time: 40 minutes

penne all'arrabbiata

■ Penne are hollow, quill-shaped pasta, available in a variety of sizes. The recipe title translation is "angry pasta quills".

hot & spicy

quick focaccia pizza with pepperoni

1 In a bowl, combine the red peppers, sun-dried tomatoes, half of the Parmesan, the cilantro or parsley, garlic, and salt and pepper.

2 Put the slices of bread onto greased baking sheets, and spread a little of the red pepper mixture over each one. Top with a few slices of pepperoni. Sprinkle with the remaining grated Parmesan and a little olive oil.

3 Bake in a preheated oven, 475°F, for about 5–10 minutes, or until bubbling. Serve hot or warm with a green salad.

■ If you cannot find bottled red peppers, you can use fresh ones but first roast them in a preheated oven, 350°F, for 20 minutes, then remove the skins and seeds.

3 bottled red peppers, drained and sliced

3 sun-dried tomatoes in oil, diced

1½ cups grated Parmesan cheese

3 tablespoons finely chopped cilantro or flat-leaf parsley

2 garlic cloves, finely chopped

12 slices focaccia or ciabatta bread

3 oz. pepperoni, thinly sliced

olive oil, for sprinkling

salt and pepper

green salad, to serve

Makes 12 focaccia pizzas
Preparation time: 10 minutes
Cooking time: 5–10 minutes

chili-topped pizza

1 Heat the oil in a pan. Add the shallots and cook for 2 minutes. Stir in the chili powder and ground beef, and cook until browned, stirring occasionally. Add the tomatoes with their juice, and the Tabasco sauce. Bring to a boil, cover, and simmer for 45 minutes, until the mixture has thickened, stirring occasionally. Remove from the heat.

2 Drain and rinse the kidney beans under cold water. Add to the pan with the garlic, and season to taste with salt and pepper. Set aside to cool.

3 Place the pizza crust on a hot baking sheet and spoon the chili mixture over it. Sprinkle the cheeses on top, and bake in a preheated oven, 425°F, for 15–20 minutes, or according to the pizza crust instructions. Serve hot.

2 tablespoons vegetable oil

4 shallots, chopped

1 teaspoon chili powder

½ lb. ground beef

1 cup canned tomatoes

dash Tabasco sauce

1 cup canned or cooked red kidney beans

1 garlic clove, crushed

1 ready-made 10-inch pizza crust

¼ lb. (around 1 cup) diced mozzarella cheese

2 teaspoons grated Parmesan cheese

salt and pepper

Serves 4
Preparation time: 10 minutes plus cooling
Cooking time: about 1¼ hours

2 tablespoons butter

2 onions, sliced

1 ready-made 10-inch pizza crust

2–3 green chiles, seeded and sliced lengthwise

1 tablespoon chopped thyme

1 tablespoon chopped marjoram

2 oz. (around ½ cup) diced mozzarella cheese

marjoram sprigs, to garnish

Tomato Sauce:

1–2 tablespoons vegetable oil

1 garlic clove, crushed

2–3 shallots, chopped

1 cup finely chopped tomatoes

⅔ cup dry white wine

1 teaspoon dried mixed Italian herbs

salt and pepper

Serves 4

Preparation time: 10 minutes plus cooling

Cooking time: about 1 hour

1 First make the tomato sauce. Heat the oil in a pan, add the garlic and shallots, and cook for about 5 minutes, or until golden. Add the tomatoes, wine, and mixed herbs. Bring to a boil and cook over a low heat for 20 minutes, until thickened. Season to taste with salt and pepper and set aside to cool.

2 Melt the butter in a pan, add the onions, and cook for 5 minutes, or until golden. Set aside to cool.

3 Put the pizza crust on a preheated baking sheet. Spread the onions on the crust and cover with the tomato sauce. Sprinkle with the chiles, thyme, marjoram, and cheese.

4 Bake in a preheated oven, 425°F, for 15–20 minutes, or according to the pizza crust instructions. Garnish with the marjoram sprigs and serve hot.

spicy hot pizza

index